Pickup Basketball
A Guide to America's Favorite Game

Ed Camp

© Copyright 2004 Ed Camp. All rights reserved.

No part of this publication may be reproduced, stored in a retrieval system, or transmitted, in any form or by any means, electronic, mechanical, photocopying, recording, or otherwise, without the written prior permission of the author.

Illustrations by Adam J. Roth

Printed in Victoria, Canada

Note for Librarians: a cataloguing record for this book that includes Dewey Classification and US Library of Congress numbers is available from the National Library of Canada. The complete cataloguing record can be obtained from the National Library's online database at: www.nlc-bnc.ca/amicus/index-e.html

ISBN 1-4120-1709-2

TRAFFORD

This book was published *on-demand* in cooperation with Trafford Publishing.
On-demand publishing is a unique process and service of making a book available for retail sale to the public taking advantage of on-demand manufacturing and Internet marketing. **On-demand publishing** includes promotions, retail sales, manufacturing, order fulfilment, accounting and collecting royalties on behalf of the author.

Suite 6E, 2333 Government St., Victoria, B.C. V8T 4P4, CANADA
Phone   250-383-6864   Toll-free   1-888-232-4444 (Canada & US)
Fax   250-383-6804   E-mail   sales@trafford.com
Web site   www.trafford.com   TRAFFORD PUBLISHING IS A DIVISION OF TRAFFORD HOLDINGS LTD.
Trafford Catalogue #03-2086   www.trafford.com/robots/03-2086.html

10   9   8   7   6   5   4   3   2   1

"Pickup Basketball" is our fond term for a game played by millions on a daily basis. Informal, unpredictable, yet essential to our lives is this game. Why, where, and who the characters are that fill ours courts consistently and earnestly day after day are explained within this very book.

Not easily explained in words, our passion for the game is so often expressed by weekly piles of sweaty tee shirts, bumps, bruises, sprains, occasional grunts, and wise-cracking conversation on and around the court. We arrange our busy schedules of family and work around our pickup games, so addictive is our sport. We come back day after day, week after week, despite the sore muscles, and upon the end of a session always look forward to the next time.

The whos, wheres, and whys of pickup basketball are attempted to be explained herein as a humorous ensemble of pictures and words, taken from real life experiences on America's urban, suburban, and rural courts.

What is Pickup Basketball: Elements that define the Game

No Referees

The principle of self-policing is a significant feature of the pickup game. It is a defining characteristic common to all unorganized athletics we arrange. Our sessions are without referees, leaving officiating to players involved in the game. This presents an often biased and sometimes amusing theatre of bad calls, misunderstandings, and darting glances amongst players making the call and those committing the foul. We quickly sort out those with intricate and not so intricate knowledge of official basketball rules. There are varying degrees of adherence to the rules of the game in the world of pickup. Some rules are intentionally overlooked while some are regularly enforced by players. The absence of referees, lets us, the pickup players, define what type of basketball we play. You might often hear, "no blood-no foul", or to the other extreme, a game very particular to the rules. This varies from court to court and is one of the key aspects of the pickup game. That being said, the following are factors we sometimes bend the rules on for the greater good of our game.

Keeping the Game Moving

Though we model our game on the structure of official basketball rules, there are certain violations that to call is to bring the game to a halt. The following are "Absolute no calls": Three second violations and carries are two of these "don't bother" calls we often let slide to keep the game moving. Calling an offensive charge is also a no-no, go for the clean block or get out of the way.

Most of us admittedly are not expert ball players, though many of us think we are. We are likely to infringe upon these rules now and then. The danger of making such a call is that it might be remembered on your team's trip down the court and handed back to you. These calls slow the game, disturbing those waiting to get next game because of the delay. Making these calls is largely viewed as "ticky-tacky" and can quickly get you labeled a total complainer (see "Complainer" in player types). Just don't do it.

Importance of the Quick Call

It is without doubt that most of us have committed one of the cardinal sins of pickup basketball – failure to make a foul call immediately. Generally speaking, the quicker a foul, out of bounds, or moving pick is called, the more likely it will be accepted by opposing players. Conversely, the late call is often met with considerable rebellion from the player or team committing the violation. The late call, in fact, has the potential to open up a Pandora's box of past plays in which no foul was called on similar plays. For those with any degree of short-term memory loss, this tactic can cause considerable challenge, and in fact causes delay in play while wits are matched. Quicker thinkers usually come out on top during these often unpleasant discourses, only to be trumped by the loudest man on the court. The best strategy to employ here is the "check ball at the top," statement, which usually is agreed upon by all parties involved, as its and result is a "no call" and play is resumed.

Game Speak

Trash-taking. Largely viewed in the world of pickup basketball as a least common denominator and a generally ugly tactic, "talking trash" can have various effects on the course of the game. A means to get in your opponents head, these sometimes overt, sometimes subtle insults can throw even the best of us off our game. Telling someone to "get that out of here" or "not in my house" after thwarting an offensive effort not only feels good, but attempts to establish one's supremacy, at least in words, to an opposing player. As a means of intimidation, trash talking can be effective on a more novice player, but can backfire on the talker if muttered to a competitive play-maker, who will either laugh it off, give it back to you, or rev him up to really take it to you on the ensuing play. Since no clear result has yet been established, trash talking is best left unsaid. Besides garnering an unpredictable outcome from the recipient, this "street method" can also potentially lead to a general ugliness throughout the game. In the event you choose trash talking, be sure to review the "Definitions" section for a colorful game speak dictionary of terms.

Giving up the Body

Hustling for a loose ball with valiant effort is one thing, laying out the body is quite another. Nothing is so appreciated by teammates than an obvious physical effort to keep a ball in bounds. Nothing can be more punishing than laying out on the court in pain going after a ball or taking a charge. Remember, we pickup players are NOT being paid for this. Competition and emotion sometimes gets the best of even the most levelheaded of us, but giving up the body is a tough call. Not recommended in this book.

Big Time Plays, Small Time Players

There have been times for all of us when we've made a no-look pass, drive to the hole and double clutch around a rising defender, fade away with the left, or make the perfect down-low up and under move, when we've felt a glimpse of greatness. Where was the camcorder at these rare moments? We develop a personal highlight reel, never to be shown on TV, but certainly to be reminisced about over and over again with those who were present at the particular moment. Hey, another eight inches and a few years taken off the birth date, and who knows? The NBA still calls in our delusional minds. Remember a few of your best plays? Sure you do. Bet you forgot about the boneheaded ones you made though. Pickup bball is like golf in the way it's the good shots that keep us coming back. Selective memory keeps us all on pedestals in our own minds. Comfortable, isn't it?

Favorite Tales of Greatness
==========================

Ah yes, how great we once all were. Pickup players (present company excluded of course) all once were shining stars of sport. How often do discussions focus on those glory days, when we were in High School, when dunking was a routine event, just another move on the court? Pickup players are like fisherman in the sense that as time goes on, that fish just keeps getting bigger. The tale can't be proved or disproved, so why not share that story about when you dunked in traffic. Someone just might believe it.

Who We Are

The pickup basketball court is loaded with people of interesting endeavor. Some of us are entrepreneurs, lawyers, students, managers, climbing the corporate ladder, falling down the corporate ladder, married, divorced, single, and some are in the dog house (not because of too much bball, of course). Part of what keeps us busy and sane is playing bball, no matter what we do in our "real " lives. Sometimes finding out what someone does as an occupation can shed some light on their game. The entrepreneur might insist on having the ball a bit more than the rest of us, while the attorney poses pungent arguments during contested calls. While the accountant might not take the ball to the hole in traffic too often, we can count on him for crisp, risk-free passes. Get rid of the nerdy glasses though!

So varied are our backgrounds in between game and after game chatting, we can learn a great deal about what is going on in another player's life. Often time, we can relate, beyond our common game to the happenings we all have experienced or will experience. Money trouble, money success; stock market tips, and stock market defeats. At times, it can all be laid out before or between games. We are, in sum, regular guys with regular lives. The niceties end though, when we get back to what we are there for, competing and challenging ourselves and others.

Aside from the occasional corporate logo tee shirt, seldom does our occupation have any identifying characteristics during game time. Regardless of industry or position, we all come to play and share equal status on the court. We can however, easily identify basketball types that nearly all of us can recognize. The following is a description of these player types and their respective thoughts. Some of which you may find humorous, but will inevitably run into sometime, hopefully not regularly, in your pickup career.

The Hacker

This slug is a low-skilled menace on the court. He'll have you bruised up in no time. Says the Hacker, "with no refs out here, I can stop anyone. Who needs skills when you can play defense like I do?" "Why give a guy a basket just because he gets by me?" The Hacker usually is a convert from wrestling or football and generously applies those physical tactics to bball without regard for fair play. The Hacker can, unfortunately change game outcome by intimidating players. When hacking gets to the point of influencing game outcome, and possibly player injury, others need to step up and set this menace straight. This guy needs to tone it down or will have to find another game to play in...perhaps even another sport altogether.

Pretty Boy

Has all the right clothes, but lacking in skills. Looks great out there, but can't claim much in the win/loss category. Pretty thinks "doesn't matter whether you win or loose, it's how good you look playing." He can be one of the worst player types to have on your team, leading to teammate frustration and possibly a trade. The indifference to the game outcome by Pretty can be almost to the point of silliness. You would think he has a model talent agency on the sidelines checking him out. Get this guy off your team as soon as possible.

Hot Shot

Doesn't say much, but can do it all on the court. Mainly seen wearing poker face, and usually anxious to get on with the game. Hot Shot says, "I'll prove who's best out here." "I might not be the biggest or strongest, but it's the fight in the dog that makes the difference." He can tend to be an over shooter or ball hog, but if the shots are falling, could be a great team asset. Hot Shot feels as though he has something to prove for whatever reason…perhaps home or work-based problems have him raring to go on the court, or simply he may have a desireable competitive spirit. Those qualities combined with a will to win slots the Hot Shot as a first pick nearly all the time.

Former DIII Player

Great guy to have on your team, but tough to defend. DIII thinks, "These un-schooled scrubs can't possibly keep up with my skills and athletic abilities." "Look at that guy, for instance....never been coached in his life." DIII might tend to be condescending and can morph into a self-appointed player-coach, much to teammates dismay. Unlike the Hot Shot, DIII's superiority complex may have him too good to exert himself on your team's behalf, hinting at a bit of a pickup bball court underachiever. The former DIII player may also have a tendency to "hang" with other A-players, assembling lopsided, nearly unstoppable teams. This tendency is unfortunate, as the stacking of teams leads to blowouts on the court. DIII would be a greater asset to the pickup session if he teamed with a few B-players and used his impressive skills to make his teammates better. The tendency of DIII to only put himself in A-player's company may have served him well in making cuts at the High

School and Collegiate level, but that left over, perhaps unconscious tactic may diminish the competitive quality of pickup games he is involved in.

The Mayor

His mouth moves faster than the feet. He has the gift of gab, most often recognized in breaks between games shaking hands and slapping backs. The Mayor thinks, " This is about networking....I've slapped more backs than you have!!" He could be selling life insurance or be a real estate broker making effort to reach his monthly sales quota. The Mayor is overall a decent guy to have around, reason being he often serves as a outside the game information resource.

The Complainer

It won't take long to recognize this beauty. Constantly stopping play for the "absolute no calls", re-tying shoes. A real eye-roller. The Complainer says "What!?!?!" "Not out on me, NO WAY!!!" Complainer, to many other's astonishment, is often so engaged in proving a point that the main focus of the game itself, and playing it, is trumped by his tirades. He may have been picked on as an adolescent.

The New Guy

No picture here, because we don't know what he looks like. Watch out for this fella. We don't know his moves, and don't expect him to let you on to any during the warm-up shoot-around. New Guy is thinking, "Wait until I lay some moves on these guys…They'll never know what hit them," and much of the time he's right....think about your success in defending someone and how dependant that success is on knowing the guy's offensive tendencies. New guy walks in – could be a friend or brother of one of the regulars, in town for the weekend – and really lights the place up, offensively. Skills may be average for your court, but the unknown factor creates points and wins for his team. Often the fellow who brought him will also pick him up when choosing teams, creating a duo who has played together before to the delight of teammates and chagrin of the opposing teams. New guy walks in with fresh new moves and leaves as one of the night's high scorers.

Thumbs Up, Thumbs Down

Though there are no written rules in the pickup bball world, there are certain unwritten aspects that we recommend, and others that we roll our eyes at. We, as a group, are reasonably accepting people, often inviting fellas to play more for the need of players than personal taste. That being said, often we end up with people playing who cross the boundaries of pickup etiquette, be it by either actions or accessories. We'll start here on a positive note, giving the nod to the following "Thumbs Up," and follow on the right with the somewhat disturbing "Thumbs Down."

Gets the Nod	Only if you need him
Black High Tops	Running/ Jogging Shoes
Old Tee Shirts	Golf/ Collared Shirts
Low Cut Socks	Knee High Socks
Crew Cuts	Pony Tails
Missing Tooth or Teeth	Mouth Guards
Prescription Goggles	Glasses
Sweatbands and Knee braces	Wearing a Wristwatch
Bringing a Camcorder	Bringing your Wife
Deodorant	B.O.
Shirts	Skins
Big Dinner after Playing	Big Dinner before Playing

Black High Tops

Industry standard footwear that make the feet look like they are moving faster than they really are. The look of black high tops or three-quarter cut sneaks also project an advanced-skill look upon the wearer, even though this may not be the truth. As a high top shoe, they also protect from ankle sprains, which really is the bottom line.

Running/ Jogging Shoes

Right off the bat this look screams "non-pickup player." We regulars know wearing jogging shoes is not only a pitiful sight, but is hazardous to the ankles. Coming down on someone else's foot with the running shoe spells Sprain City. We've seen people roll over on ankles, and its not a pretty sight

Old Tee Shirts

Another pickup standard. Tee shirts are perhaps the most versatile sporting wear available to man. Shirts with car repair or landscaping services displayed are preferable, brand name athletic sporting goods logos are certainly acceptable, while corporate logos or family reunion logos are frowned upon. The tee shirt also prevents your nasty sweat from being rubbed off on others...until it's completely soaked from all the running around. To remedy this situation, be sure to bring along some extra shirts.

Skins

Absence of a shirt typically is used in pickup to distinguish one team from another. Though effective in this sense, skins present a myriad of problems to the opposing team. Most obviously, there is no shirt to absorb player sweat. Instead, the defensive man often finds himself sliding against sweaty chests and backs. Skins gives literal meaning to "sliding by' your defender. Additionally, the typical shirtless 30+ year old pickup player is nothing to gawk at either...the belly hanging over the pant waistline is anything but inspirational. Its just plain nasty bumping into that walrus gut. Keep the shirts on and play ball.

Golf Collared Shirts

Though better than skins, the golf shirt reeks of non-player status. Those who adorn the golf shirt wear a virtual "post me up and run me silly" sign on their forehead. Not a play inhibitor, but truly sends a message…and the wrong one at that. Golf shirts belong on the course, in the office, or around town, definitely not on the basketball court. Way too preppy for a hard-core game like pickup.

Low Cut Socks

Popular originally among tennis players in the 1980's, low cut socks have become commonplace on America's bball courts. They keep the feet dry, as normal socks do, but allow the calves to display their awesome musculature. Not!

Knee High Socks

No denying knee-highs have become popular at the college and professional levels. This throwback look evokes memories of the stylish 1970's when anything went. The knee-high look works hand-in-hand with the Afro and red, white, and blue basketball. If that is your style, so be it. Have fun constantly pulling them back up during the course of the game. Oh, and if you wear the accompanying

Afro, don't keep a comb in it, it'll fall out. The Afro may also be hazardous while playing outdoor ball during an approaching thunderstorm, as it is a prime conductor of static electricity.

Pony Tails

Great segway from the Afro conversation…Also a frowned upon look. Depending on length, a ponytail can literally get in the way of your game. You may inadvertently rope yourself while making a lay up, or worse yet, hog-tie the next guy with that thing swinging around.

Crew Cuts

Ah, the standard crew cut gets the thumbs up for so many reasons. They evoke an intense, no-frills look, they keep hair out of the eyes, a crew cut feels cool when you rub the guy's head after a nice play, and somehow, masks male pattern baldness. Crew cuts seem to make you look more athletic and thinner, and somehow make you <u>feel</u> thinner as well. That feeling alone has been known to have positive effects on many a pickup player's game, seemingly allowing him to jump higher and run faster.

<u>Missing Tooth or Teeth</u>

In general, an awesome sports look. The guy with this deficit is nearly always an asset to your team. Add in the slightly crazed look in the eye and a smile and you have basically the complete player. The look speaks volumes on the guy's brazenness and cavalier outlook on not just the game but life itself.

Mouth Guards/ Teeth Protectors

Presents the problem of a player "keeping himself healthy." No one wants a guy on his team who is concerned about cosmetic appearances. We want the player who is messy and angry on our squad. Though the mouth guard makes sense, we prefer missing teeth, but if you have to wear one, get it dyed in some wild color like red or yellow.

Prescription Goggles

If you can't deal with contact lenses and your vision is such that without prescriptive aid you just can't play to your full capability, goggles are the way to go. They stay on if harnessed with the elastic strap, and even have the added benefit of protecting the eyes from all those swiping hands as you take it to the hoop.

Glasses

Glasses have multiple drawbacks…they constantly fall off, can cut the face if you get hit by a ball or a body, and give the player a nerdly wiz-kid look. You also run the risk of having them crushed once they fall off if play doesn't stop immediately, which it seldom does. Get some goggles or contact lenses before you step on our court.

Sweatbands and Knee braces

Non verbal way of saying "been there, done that." These simple and practical devices give the wearer a "battle-worn" look, not to mention support for the knees and also function to keep stinging seat off the brow and out of the eyes.. Knee braces in particular evoke a sense among players that the bearer of the brace is a multi-sport athlete, who perhaps took a big hit to the knee in his earlier years as a running back.

Wearing a wristwatch

There is no way you need to know exactly what time it is while playing. Besides becoming a player-scratching object, those who wear wristwatches remind us of the geek on our little league team who could not be separated from his digital pal.

Bringing a camcorder

Highly recommended bring-along tool to film you and the boys hot-dogging and having fun. You might just catch a pal making one of those highlight reel moves, or be lucky enough to have someone waiting filming you doing the same. With the rewind and slow motion capabilities of VCRs, the laughs could be endless. Pop it in at work, at family gatherings (after some skillful editing of course) sit the nephews down and let them gaze at uncle's bball prowess. While filming, be sure to use the zoom in when you sense a big play coming on. Capture the hilarity of the game and it's characters.

Bringing the Wife

Or girlfriend, just not at the same time. Definite thumbs down on this foolhardy decision. With significant other in attendance, we introduce the combination of her being bored out of her mind, and you exerting yourself beyond average effort. The natural tendency we speak of here is for anyone with an audience to try too hard. The balance of the game will be off kilter and she will have a headache from all the yelling. She may end up with another sweaty guy yapping to her while waiting and can become completely turned off by the whole thing. Better to keep our secret to ourselves.

Deodorant

Anyone forgetting to put deodorant on in the morning may get away with it during the workday, but will subject us all to a real stench an hour or more into playing. Smell becomes especially pronounced is an unwashed tee shirt is worn during the run. Player may find stinky self alone a lot.

Chowing down before playing may really slow you down on the court and cramp up the abdomen. It's hard to resist that pre-session meatloaf, but all your exertion will bring back meatloaf memories you don't want to have.

Big Dinner After Playing

A nice way to cap off the evening of exercise is a large Chinese dinner with plenty of fried rice, sauces, and pork. The carbos from the rice and sodium from everything else will leave you with a pronounced stomach and a subtle smile on your face. Be sure to fold the arms across your chest, resting them on top of the belly for a nice Buddha look.

Definitions

All Ball – expression usually used during a debate over a foul call during a blocked shot. Insinuates that there was not foul committed and that literally only the ball was blocked by the defender, and not body part of the shooter was touched.

Check Ball – Stop game action, bring ball to the top of the key, ready offense and defense and resume play.

Shoot for Ball – A player is to shoot from beyond the three-point line to determine which team begins offensive play.

Get Outta my House – Typically used by defensive player after blocking a shot. Often exclaimed with great enthusiasm in or near face of player making attempt at scoring.

Cherry Picker – Player who remains under his offensive basket while his team is on the other end of the court playing defense. The cherry picker seeks to gather the outlet pass after his hard-working team grabs a defensive rebound and make an easy lay up. May also be categorized as one who is "Dogging It," for lack of defensive effort.

En Fuego – Great sports expression used to describe player who just can't miss. Literal translation, "on fire!"

Shake it Off – Said to a player who suffers a minor injury. Expression is most often used when injured player is needed for even sides and not replaceable ie: five-on-five.

The Zone – A nearly magical physical and mental state rarely visited by pickup players, in which impossible shot attempts gain nothing but net. This state is reserved for top-level players, but we have seen brief instances of a pickup player entering and playing in the Zone.

<u>Why We Play</u>

The answer is simple. Desk jobs. Sitting in from of a computer most of the day is the common denominator most of us share regardless of field of employment. We site in cars, buses, trains, and subways to get to work, then spend most if our at-work time sitting in meetings or at desks. Our daily caloric consumption far outpaces the fifty calories burnt clicking a mouse and drinking coffee all day. For the typical 30+ year old pickup basketball player, the equation is ugly...if not for our once, twice, or three time a week run around the court, we'd be whales with legs.

What is the alternative? Aerobics or a treadmill? We'd rather live the thrill of competition and bumping into other sweaty guys for a few hours a week.

OK, Seriously, the Competition

Matching physical and mental skills with other athletes surely is a thrill. Most of us pickup players experienced this competition in high school or college athletic teams, or by merely watching them. We seek to continuously challenge ourselves to rise to the occasion of game time. We all have personal benchmarks we can measure ourselves to and improve upon through pickup basketball. As competitive people, we enjoy the competition we experience in our games, and we challenge each other to keep ourselves sharp and strong in our otherwise soft, politically correct lives. We can be ourselves out on the court, so back to our animal instincts, all within the rules of a civil game of course, we run again with a pack. We've all been there when competitive spirits get out of hand. An occasional shoving match might occur, hopefully ending quickly with handshakes and a quick return to play.

The Camaraderie

In these busy days of juggling work and family, scheduling even the briefest meeting with friends is often difficult. We need a regular meeting place. What's more, we need a regular meeting time, place, and enjoyable activity to balance our over committed lives. A place for us to vent and pal around with fellows of similar age range and interests. We enjoy seeing these familiar faces in our sometimes stranger-filled world. We mix basketball with brief but meaningful conversation about our daily lives and ideas, and find comfort in knowing we can pick up where we left off a few days or weeks later with our fellow bball enthusiasts. Sometimes we begin a pickup league or open gym with a friend, often we develop new friendships over the course of a season. Many of these friendships last for years. Over time, not only do we learn each other's fade-away and pump fake moves, we establish who we are as people beyond the game. Bringing a non-regular friend can be fun, especially if he is good and on your team. See "the New Guy" for further commentary on this game time wildcard.

The Beer after the game

What would a workout be without completely negating it with a beer fest afterward? This best occurs during mid Fall and early Winter, where at least on the East Coast, the second half of Monday night Football can be watched with fellow pickup players at the closest establishment. The only outstanding debate is whether to arrive in gym clothes or go home to change first. We'll let the reader decide. In late winter and early Spring, basketball may serve as the focal point. Any sport is fine for that matter, as long as its not soccer.

Getting out of the House

After a lazy day at work, pickup basketball gets us out of the house, away from some familial pressures and into the company of "athletes." Not to be used as a vehicle to skirt responsibilities, but as a means of temporary relief from them. A brief hiatus of sorts, pickup basketball returns us to moments in time when we had little to be worried about besides our own well-being. As a break or downtime from our ever-increasing responsibilities, pickup helps to give us our necessary self-time, while in the company of others perusing the same. Just don't forget to take the trash out when you get home. If you miss the can, follow shot and rebound.

Spin-off Sports

Mainly golf and softball. We already have the background with each other, so it's easy to set up town or company – sponsored softball squads. Ditto for golf. Spin-off sports also let us test each other in other sport talents. New hierarchies can also develop in the other sports, as we all know the top dog on the basketball court may not retain his status on the golf links. Flag football is another one we enjoy, but beware of conflicts with the pickup bball scheduling.

Types of Pickup Games

Three on three. Usually played when not enough fellows show up to run and full-court game. "Threes" is usually played in a half-court setting, and showcases individual player skills more so than the team-oriented full court game. We often look to playing threes while waiting for more players to show up, and then quickly wrap up the game once they do show. Counting shots made behind the three-point line tends to open things up and often adds some strategy to the three on three format. Especially when played as a time killer, a three on three game can lead to non-chalant play, with only the most motivated players actually exerting any real effort.

Four-on four. The quicker man's dream game is four on four. The openness of playing full court with only four men to a team serves the smaller, quicker player well. Plenty of open court provides excellent passing and rebounding opportunities for the average-sized player.

Five-on-five. A true full court game utilizing the maximum number of players per team the game of basketball allows. Passes have to be crisp and on the mark as lanes close quickly with this many players on defense. Big men exert more influence in the fives game, as less room under the basket has them control most of the rebounding. Finish the night with fives if at all possible. Loosing two players and going with four on four ends up being a lazy game, with little hustling up and down the court.

Where We Play

Regular pickup games can take place anywhere there is at least a half court and a basket. For full court, schoolyards, school gyms, indoors or outdoors will work for us. There are pluses and minuses to both. If you are an outside shooter, you can be deterred by an outdoor court, as sun and wind factors might throw your marksmanship-like shot off. The indoor gyms generally cancel those inhibiting factors out, and provide a "truer" bounce floor, better backboards and rims, and some temperature control. If you are lucky enough to have a nicely paved outdoor court with great weather, you are either real lucky or didn't have an indoor gym to play in to start with. We are a lucky group after all, and are sure to catch a weather break now and then.

Some swear by the outdoor court game, others are strictly gym rats. Here is a closer look at the breakdown between indoor vs. outdoor:

Outdoor Pros	Outdoor Cons	Indoor Pros	Indoor Cons
Sun	Weather dependant	Good floor	Not always available
Always Open	Poor Pavement	Nice rims	Too expensive
	Chain nets	Glass backboards	
	No nets		
	Wind		

When We Play

Though pickup games can break out at nearly any moment provided enough people and a basketball are around a court, most often the best games occur during regular weekly, bi weekly, or tri weekly scheduled times. Reason being, we can count on enough showing up to run full court. Times of the day vary, however, and are usually early morning, lunchtime, or evening/ night.

Early Morning – This is reserved for the strictly insane, or simply for those who cannot get out at the more reasonable times. Some say it "gives you an edge" through the rest of the day, and that in itself is of value. I couldn't imagine much friendly banter occurring at the break of dawn. On the positive side, not much complaining either.

Lunch Hour – Might be a little bit rushed, since by nature most of us do not have much time for lunch. Perhaps this break is exactly that...a break from and invigoration for the remainder of the workday. There have better be a shower nearby, or you may not be talked to upon returning to the workplace. Well, maybe that is the idea anyway!

Night – This is Showtime. The workday is over, the players come out, and everyone is jacked-up. We've had all day to think about getting out there and making plays, making a difference. A lot of enthusiasm rushes on to the court during the night sessions. It's "our" time, hopefully outside responsibilities have been set aside for now. No clock-watching here, night pickup bball can go for hours and hours, sometimes extending until we simply tire out, left to nearly crawling home.

Have Ball, Will Travel

How far have you traveled for a pickup session you know would be a good run? By subway, car, bus, or by foot, we make our way to get in on a good game. The anticipation of playing can last an entire day, and propels us to travel sometimes nearly insane distances to play. Obviously, the closer the court, the better, and bring a change of clothes if you are taking public transportation home. It's upsetting enough to play with a sweaty guy, never mind sitting or standing beside one on a crowded bus or subway. If you leave without a basketball, make sure you have some other means of explaining your mess so people don't think you just ran from robbing a bank or something.

Pickup Everywhere

Even on vacations or business trips we can find pickup sessions occurring nearly anywhere. The chance to keep the skills up while away from your home court is made possible by the mere presence of an indoor or outdoor court. Follow up your playing with a dive in the pool or lake....now that's a business trip!

Pickup Player's Guide to Favorite Off-Court Activities

When we are not playing, pickup players are enjoying a variety of activities. Cell Biology, no, we're talking about some real low-effort stuff here. Playing pickup is strenuous, here are several of our low-strain favorites.

TV- What to Watch, How to Watch

Sports commentating and analysis shows have experienced a recent boom on TV. They have proliferated to our delight, so when we are not watching actual games we can pick up insight and a few laughs from the cast of former coaches and players who sunset their on-field careers into a commentating television slot. Not only are the programs great stand-alone entertainment, but the commercials, geared toward guys like us, can be creative and sometimes hilarious.

Internet

One of man's greatest inventions, the internet allows us to surf through vast stores of sports statistics, schedules, real-time scores, and generally allows us to be sports spectators nearly anytime, from anywhere. With the rising popularity of internet video, we can watch highlight reel hoops, amazing touchdown catches, and on-court brawls all from a cushy desk chair at home. Your home-based email is also a perfect resource for communicating and setting up pickup games with your fellow players.

Fantasy Sports

Whether it be via Internet or office pool, fantasy sports teams makes us feel as if we have some influence over the games. Selecting and trading pro stars is thrill enough, but watching and tracking their performance day to day is a lot of fun. The thrill of competing with pals around the office or from your favorite hangout is terrific. Statistics galore here.

Eating

Perhaps the favorite non-sport activity in the pickup player's world, eating serves as not only a culinary delight, but an outlet for our natural aggression. Excessiveness in this hobby of course can run counter to our playing aspirations, as the weight gain consequence of plowing food down might keep you below the rim. The following are descriptions of some favorite culinary choices:

Grilling in the backyard

Cooking up some meats on the grill can be awesome fun on a nice day. There is nothing like enjoying the outdoors and grilling on a mild summer weekend. Marinating your meat of choice is highly recommended before grilling, as are the "second lieutenants" of the grilling General, barbeque sauce and beer. Set up the TV alongside the grill with sports on, and you've scored the hat trick.

Chinese

The ease of home delivery, the charm of the Chinese restaurant workers, and the delightful taste of rice with anything you can imagine, makes Chinese food a pickup player's supper standby. With little to no home preparation required, Chinese food can go straight from delivery bag to mouth, using a fork, of course. Don't pay any mind to those chopsticks they package in with your meal.

Mexican

The zestful, festive nature of Mexico is captured in a well-prepared Mexican meal. The sheer size and weight of some Mexican dinner plate items make it one of the pickup player's favorite dinners. Any spicy melted cheese medley ranks high on our choicest food menus.

Fruit Dish

The cool, sugary fruit dish is another staple of the pickup player's diet. The healthiness of this meal will keep you in fighting shape. Just kidding.

Pickup Basketball, Our Game

Whether it's the city, suburbs, or the countryside, millions of us enjoy this predictable, yet unpredictable game week-in and week-out. We play in varied court settings, we bring a world of personalities, we arrive from varied locations, and have varied expectations of ourselves and others come game time. We are varied in our backgrounds, occupations, race, and place of origin, but are bonded in our love for the sport.

We need each other for the competition, the camaraderie, and most basically, to play the game. The need for numbers to complete two teams is paramount, and that need requires us to be a tolerant bunch. We put up with and have to get along with the lack of refereeing, the complex personalities, and the scale of age and skill levels to make the game possible. That is after all, what it is all about in pickup….giving ourselves the chance to play. Chances are, if you've played pickup, you can relate to at least some parts of this descriptive book. Keep on playing, showcasing your talents, while doing battle on America's pickup courts.

Pickup Basketball Resources

www.biggamesmallworld.com

Author Bio – Ed Camp

"Multi-dimensional game, steady competitor, level-headed enough to make the observations contained within this book WHILE actually playing the game. A regular in North Jersey's open gyms.

Illustrator Bio – Adam J. Roth

Average sized guy with a big-man's presence. Has elements of the Hacker and the Mayor in his game, but is truly a multi-dimensional team asset. An East Coast native, AJ now resides in Pasadena, California and still finds opportunity to play AND illustrate, just not at the same time.

ISBN 141201709-2